Arctic Ocean

Asia

Europe

China

India

Africa

Indian Ocean

Australia

Southern Ocean

Antarctica

China

Leonie Pratt

Designed by Josephine Thompson
and Abigail Brown

Illustrated by Emmanuel Cerisier

Additional illustrations by Ruth Rivers
China consultant: Dr. Paul Bailey, University of Edinburgh
Reading consultant: Alison Kelly, Roehampton University

Contents

Old and new

China is a country with a long and exciting history, where old traditions are still part of life today.

This old boat, called a junk, is sailing into the modern city of Hong Kong.

Big country

China is one of the biggest countries in the world. More people live there than in any other country.

The deserts in the north are hot in the day and cold at night.

The Yangtze is China's longest river.

In the west there are tall mountains and windy plains.

This is Mount Everest, the highest mountain in the world.

China's full name is the People's Republic of China. This is its flag.

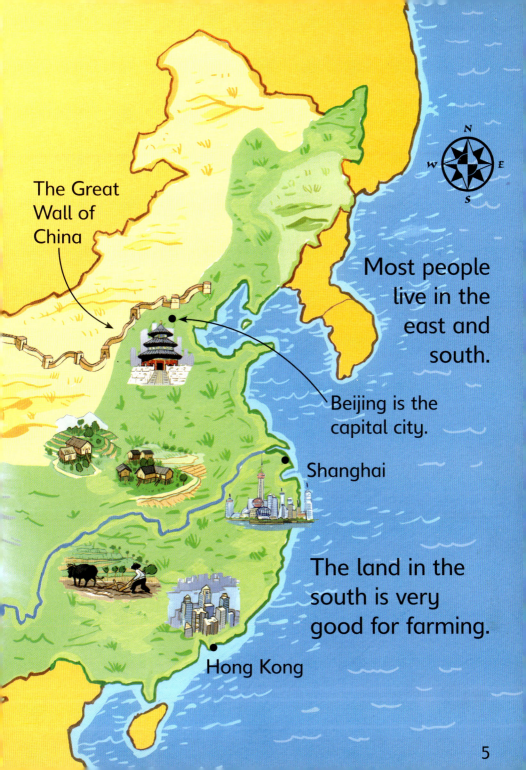

The Great
Wall of
China

Most people
live in the
east and
south.

Beijing is the
capital city.

Shanghai

The land in the
south is very
good for farming.

Hong Kong

5

Emperors rule

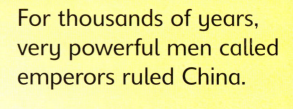

For thousands of years, very powerful men called emperors ruled China.

This is a picture of Emperor Taizong, who ruled China from 626 to 649.

His yellow robes show that he is important. Ordinary people did not wear yellow.

China had hundreds of emperors, but Wu Zeitan was the only female emperor.

The emperor lived in his palace, making rules and running the country.

People had to pass special exams so they could work for the emperor as mandarins.

Mandarins lived all over China and made sure people followed the emperor's laws.

Keep out!

The first emperor built the Great Wall of China over 2,000 years ago. Later emperors added to it and parts of it still stand today.

The wall was built to stop armies from the north invading China.

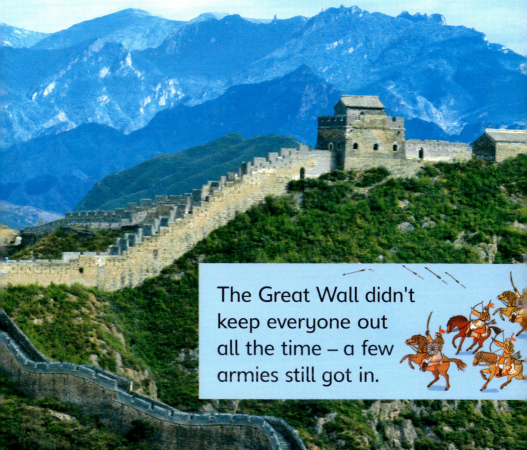

If a lookout spotted an enemy, he lit a smoky fire on top of a tower as a signal.

The signal went from tower to tower, warning soldiers to get ready to fight.

The Great Wall didn't keep everyone out all the time – a few armies still got in.

Chinese art

Paintings that are hundreds of years old tell us what life was like in ancient China.

There are many pictures of different emperors and life in their palaces.

Some artists painted scenes from nature, such as landscapes, animals and flowers.

This very old painting shows people bringing horses as gifts for the emperor.

Many old paintings are on very long scrolls that can be rolled out.

Chinese pottery was decorated with beautiful patterns of flowers and animals.

Dragons meant power, and were only used to decorate the emperor's things.

By land and by sea

Chinese people discovered how to make many things that people from other countries wanted to buy.

Soft material called silk.

Beautiful china.

A hot drink called tea.

Many of these goods were carried over mountains and deserts on camels.

The Chinese also transported huge loads in big ships called junks. Junks like the one in this painting sailed to Africa and India.

Sailors hung red flags from their masts, to please the dragons they believed lived in the sea.

Life goes on...

The Chinese believed that when people died, their spirits lived on in another world.

A body was carried in a covered box to a specially built tomb.

People left gifts at the tomb for the spirit to use in the spirit world.

They thought that gifts made from jade gave the spirit a long life.

Qingming is a festival when people visit their ancestors' graves and sweep them clean.

These statues are part of a huge terracotta army in Emperor Qin's tomb. They were put there to protect him in the spirit world.

Change in China

100 years ago most people in China were poor, starving and unhappy with the emperor.

People turned against the young emperor, Pu Yi, and made him give up his power.

Two different groups wanted to rule in his place. They fought each other for control.

In 1949, the Chinese Communist Party led by Mao Zedong, took control of the country.

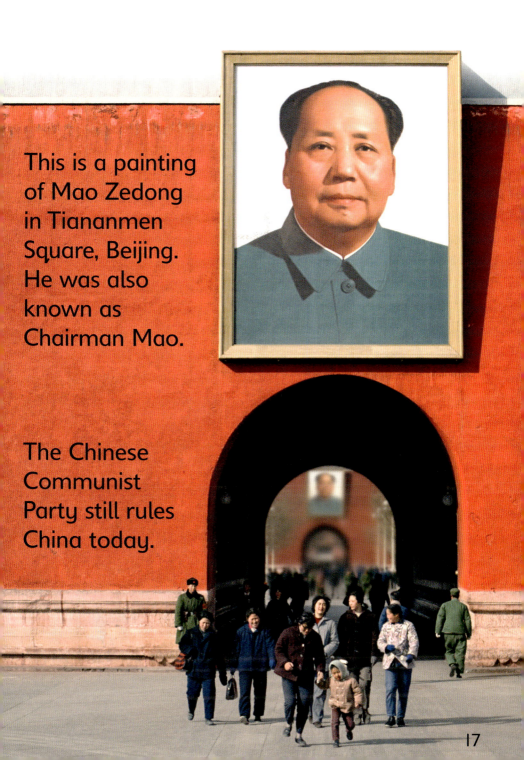

This is a painting of Mao Zedong in Tiananmen Square, Beijing. He was also known as Chairman Mao.

The Chinese Communist Party still rules China today.

City life

Some of the world's busiest cities are in China. This is a street in Shanghai, China's biggest city.

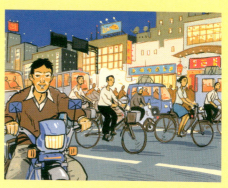

There isn't a lot of space, so whole families live together.

Lots of people use bicycles to get from place to place.

Big groups of people go to parks to do an exercise called tai chi.

Kite-flying is popular in China, especially on public holidays.

Tiananmen Square, in Beijing, is the biggest square in the world.

Food for families

Family life is very important and meals are a good time for everyone to get together.

Everyone takes food from dishes in the middle of the table.

It's polite for older family members to start eating first.

People lift up their bowls and eat their food with chopsticks.

Everyone pours tea for the person sitting next to them.

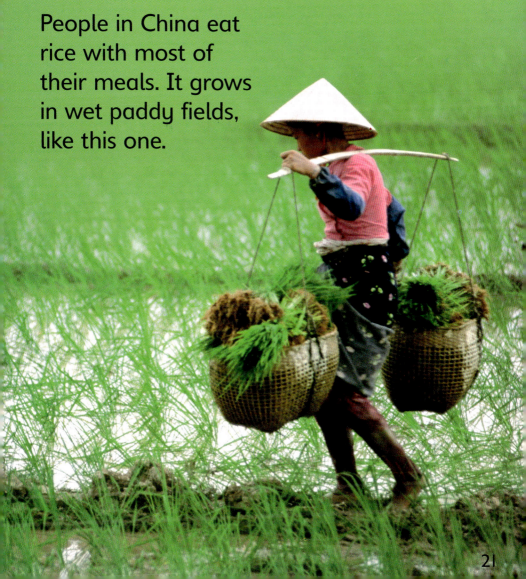

Noodles are a symbol of long life, and are often part of a birthday meal.

People in China eat rice with most of their meals. It grows in wet paddy fields, like this one.

Beautiful words

Chinese words are not made up of letters. Instead, each word is written as a symbol.

Some symbols were once pictures of things:

hill   eye   person

Today, these symbols are more simple:

hill   eye   person

Sometimes, two different symbols are put together to make a new word:

sun   moon   bright

Calligraphy is the art of writing beautifully, using a special brush.

The tip of the brush is made from animal fur.

Ink is made from
black soot and glue.
It is mixed with water on
an inkstone before being used.

Chinese New Year

New Year is the biggest Chinese holiday.
It celebrates the start of spring, in late
January or February.
The festival lasts
for fifteen days.

Houses are swept,
ready for the holiday.

All the family meet
on New Year's Eve.

People set off noisy
firecrackers outside.

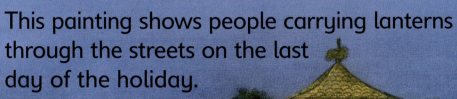

This painting shows people carrying lanterns
through the streets on the last
day of the holiday.

Lion and dragon dances bring good luck.

Buddhism

Buddhism is the most popular religion in China. Buddhists believe that people will be born into a new life after they die.

Buddhists also believe in karma. Do good things, and good things will happen to you.

People visit temples to pray and burn sticks of incense as offerings to the spirits.

Monks spend time being quiet and relaxing their minds. They are meditating.

This big statue of Buddha is in Hong Kong.

Visitors have to climb 268 steps to see the statue close up.

Living in the wild

There are lots of unusual animals living all over China.

Golden-haired monkeys live in tropical forests.

Water deer live near rivers. They have small tusks.

Rare porpoises nicknamed 'river pigs' live in the Yangtze.

Flocks of red-crowned cranes gather on China's lakes.

Giant pandas live on China's mountain slopes. There are very few pandas left in the wild – only about 1,600.

Pandas spend most of the day sitting or lying down while they eat bamboo.

Glossary of China words

Here are some of the words in this book you might not know. This page tells you what they mean.

 emperor - a powerful ruler. Emperors ruled China until 1911.

 mandarin - someone who worked for the emperor.

 jade - a gemstone that is often green or white. It's believed to bring long life.

 tai chi - an exercise where people do a series of certain moves very slowly.

 chopsticks - long thin sticks used to pick up food.

 firecrackers - loud fireworks meant to scare off evil spirits at New Year.

 incense - a powder that burns slowly and gives off a nice smell.

Websites to visit

If you have a computer, you can find out more about China on the internet. On the Usborne Quicklinks Website there are links to four fun websites.

Website 1 - Learn some Chinese phrases.

Website 2 - Watch a video about pandas.

Website 3 - Find out your Chinese star sign.

Website 4 - Prepare for New Year in a fun game.

To visit these websites, go to **www.usborne-quicklinks.com** Read the internet safety guidelines, and then type the keywords "beginners china".

The websites are regularly reviewed and the links in Usborne Quicklinks are updated. However, Usborne Publishing is not responsible, and does not accept liability, for the content or availability of any website other than its own. We recommend that children are supervised while on the internet.

These pottery animals are 'roof guardians'. They were put there to protect the emperor's palace in Beijing from evil spirits and fires.

Index

Acknowledgements

Map illustration front end paper by Craig Asquith, European Map Graphics Ltd.
Cover design by Zoe Wray. Photographic manipulation by Nick Wakeford.

Photo credits
The publishers are grateful to the following for permission to reproduce material:
© The Art Archive / Bibliothèque des Arts Décoratifs Paris/Alfredo Dagli Orti 1; © The Art Archive/Bibliothèque Nationale Paris 12; © The Art Archive/Eileen Tweedy 13; © The Festival of the Lanterns, pub. by Formentin, 1824-27 (litho), French School, (19th century)/Stapleton Collection, UK./The Bridgeman Art Library 24-25; © Freer Gallery of Art, Smithsonian Institution, Washington, D.C. Gift of Charles Lang Freer, F1915.16 10-11; © Image Source/Photolibrary Group 27; © JUSTIN GUARIGLIA/National Geographic Image Collection cover; © Keren Su/China Span 8-9; © Michael S. Yamashita/CORBIS 21; © Nik Wheeler/CORBIS 2-3; © PanoramaStock/ Robert Harding 29; © Pierre Colombel/CORBIS 6; © Ric Ergenbright/CORBIS 31; © SCPhotos/Alamy 18; © Steve Vidler/SuperStock 14-15; © Ursula Gahwiler/Robert Harding 17; © View Stock/Alamy 23

 Sun, Moon and Stars

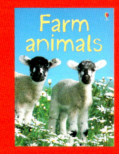 Farm animals

 Elizabeth I

 TRASH AND RECYCLING

 Dogs

 Horses and ponies

 Spiders

 Planes

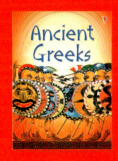 Ancient Greeks

 Cats

 VOLCANOES

 DINOSAURS

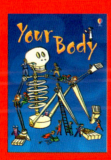 Your Body

 Armor

 Sharks

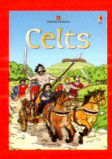 Celts

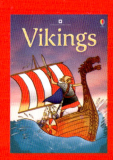

Vikings

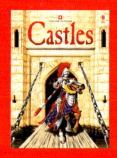

Castles

How flowers grow

Knights

Living in space

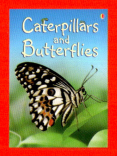

Caterpillars and Butterflies

Ballet

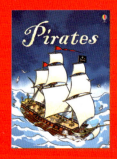

Pirates

Egyptians

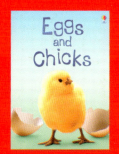

Eggs and Chicks

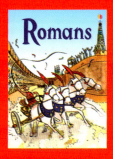

Romans

Weather

Tadpoles and frogs

Why do we eat?

Under the sea

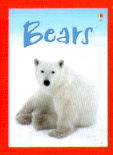

Bears